MARY

Get to Know Series

Nancy I. Sanders

ZONDER**kidz**

MARY

Nancy I. Sanders

ZONDERKIDZ

Mary
Copyright © 2014 by Nancy I. Sanders
Cover illustration © 2014 by Greg Call

This title is also available as a Zondervan ebook.
Visit www.zondervan.com/ebooks.

Requests for information should be addressed to:

Zonderkidz, *3900 Sparks Dr., Grand Rapids, Michigan 49546*

ISBN 978-0-310-74480-1

Ronnie Ann Herman, Herman Agency

Cover design: Cindy Davis
Interior design: David Conn and Ben Fetterley

Printed in China

14 15 16 17 18 19 DSC 20 19 18 17 16 15 14 13 12 11 10 9 8 7 6 5 4 3 2 1

Dedication

To Gertrude Toppin—at 94 the sweetness
of Christ radiates from your ever-present smile
just as brightly as ever!

ACKNOWLEDGMENTS

I want to thank first and foremost my husband, Jeff. As a fourth grade teacher, you always provide invaluable input into each one of my children's books, including this one! Thanks also to our wonderful sons Dan and Ben (and your new bride Christina!). Dad and I count our blessings daily because of each of you.

Thanks to Ronnie Herman, my agent extraordinaire! For your help, for your guidance, for your hard work, and for your love of birds and everything green and growing. You're a treasured gem in my life!

Also a big thank you to editor Mary Hassinger, Annette Bourland, and all the amazingly wonderful folks at Zonderkidz. What an exciting journey this series has been to work on together.

Thank you to Pastor Jack and Lisa Hibbs and for your commitment to speak the truth about the Bible and the teachings of Jesus Christ. I also want to thank Charlie H. Campbell, a frequent speaker at our church and the author of reliable information about faith, history, and the Bible. May the truth taught set the record straight about the trustworthiness of the Scriptures for this generation and those to come.

TABLE
OF CONTENTS

A Daughter in the House of Jacob 11

Engaged to Be Married...19

Birth of the Firstborn Son....................................... 27

The Newborn King.. 35

The Town of Nazareth.. 43

Mary and Joseph's Home 49

Sharing Faith with Her Family 55

Holidays are Holy Days..61

Life and Death.. 69

Dealing with the Messiah 75

At the Cross 83

A New Beginning.. 89

Timeline of Mary 96

Glossary 99

Selected Bibliography...105

Source Notes...107

Student Resources.. 111

About the Author 112

GET TO KNOW ... THIS BOOK

The Get to Know series is all about Bible heroes and the time period in which they lived. Each book in the series provides information about a person whose life and work impacts the world and Bible times. To help you understand everything in these books, we have provided features to help you recognize important information and facts.

SCRIPTURE

Look for an oil lamp to read a Scripture from the Bible.

BIBLE HERO

Look for a sandal for information about a Bible hero.

EYEWITNESS ACCOUNT

Look for a picture of an eye each time someone who saw what happened tells about it.

DID YOU KNOW?

Look for a clay jar to learn fun facts.

WORD BANK

Look for a scroll to learn the meanings of new words. The words are also in bold on the page.

Chapter 1

A DAUGHTER IN THE HOUSE OF JACOB

Have you ever seen a **nativity** set at Christmas? It is usually a model of some type of building or cave. There is a mother named Mary. There is a father named Joseph. There might be a shepherd with his sheep. Sometimes there are figures of kings riding on camels. And sometimes there are angels hovering nearby. Everyone is looking at a little baby named Jesus.

A nativity set is a common sight at Christmas.

Artville

Nativity: The birth of Jesus

A nativity set often has a **stable**, a kind of barn, possibly with a cow and donkey inside. There might be bales of hay. Usually, baby Jesus is sleeping on a bed of straw in a box that holds food for the animals, called a **manger**.

© William D. Mounce

A manger held food for cows, sheep, goats, and donkeys.

A nativity scene shows the place Jesus was born. But a Nativity set does not show the whole picture of Jesus' birth. It does not show Bethlehem, the village where Jesus was born. It does not show the big crowds of people who had traveled to Bethlehem to be counted in a **census**.

It does not show Roman soldiers who were in Bethlehem to help count the people living in the Roman Empire.

A nativity set does not show King Herod the

Stable: Barn for animals

Manger: Box that holds food for animals

Census: An official count of people living in a certain place

Great—the king ruling over the whole area or Caesar Augustus—the **emperor** who ruled over the Roman Empire at the time. He was the one who ordered everyone to be counted.

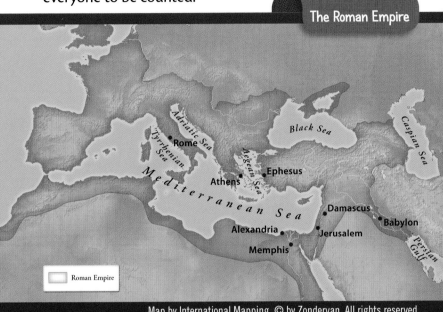

The Roman Empire

Rome ruled the world at that time. Roman soldiers conquered cities and even entire nations. Great battles were fought on land and sea. Everyone had to obey the commands of Caesar and his mighty Roman warriors.

Emperor: The ruler over a group of countries

Even a young woman named Mary had to obey
these men. This is the same Mary in the Nativity set—
Mary, the mother of baby Jesus. We don't know much
specific information about this Mary. The little we
do know is found in the Bible. However, we do know
a lot about the world Mary lived in. History is full of
treasures from the place and time that she lived. So to
learn more about Mary we have to study about when
and where she lived.

Mary was probably born around 20 BC. She lived in
the town of Nazareth in Galilee.

Judea, Samaria, and Galilee were three areas in the
Roman Empire. This is part of the world that is the
country of Israel today. And this was where a special
group of people lived. They were the Jews—God's
chosen people.

The Jews already had a long, rich history by the
time Mary was born. One of the most well-known
Jewish **ancestors** was a man named Jacob. Long ago,
God changed Jacob's name to Israel. He had twelve
sons. Each of these sons became one of the leaders of
the twelve **tribes** or families of Israel. Judah was one of
those tribes of Israel.

Ancestors: Parents, grandparents, and older people
in a family
Tribes: Different groups within the same family

A boy named David was born into the tribe of Judah. This was one thousand years before Mary was born. David grew up to be a great king in Israel. As king he made Jerusalem the **capital** city of Israel and formed all twelve tribes into one powerful kingdom. Years later, other kingdoms conquered Israel. And then one day, Rome became the ruler over the Jews.

Mary was a Jew. As a little girl, she learned all about her family's faith. She went to the **synagogue** with her family. The synagogue was a special place Jews met each Saturday for worship and prayer. Mary heard the Scriptures read aloud at the synagogue. These Scriptures were writings in the Old Testament, the Jewish holy book of faith.

Mary probably didn't go to a school. In Bible times, only boys went to school. Mary got most of her education at home but it probably did not include lessons in reading, writing, or math. Mothers taught their daughters how to cook and clean and care for their home and family.

Mary and her family celebrated seven main feasts every year. These feasts were considered holidays and were very holy to the Jewish people.

Capital: City where the leader rules
Synagogue: Building where Jews meet for worship

Ruins of a synagogue from the fourth century AD

Wikimedia Commons

One feast Mary's family celebrated each year was Passover. They remembered how long ago God delivered the Israelites out of slavery in Egypt with the help of Moses. Now they looked for a **Messiah** to deliver them again, this time from harsh Roman rule.

Many of the Scriptures talked about a coming Messiah. He would be sent from God. He would be born into the tribe of Judah and would save the Jews. It was part of God's plan begun in the time of Adam and Eve, the first people God created.

Mary lived in a time of political **unrest**. The Jews did not want Roman soldiers marching through their streets. They did not want to pay heavy taxes to Rome. These taxes were monies that went to the leaders like Caesar, and the people could not always afford them.

Messiah: The promised Savior of the Jews

Unrest: Unhappy people, often in regard to leadership

Most Jews hoped the Messiah would set them free from Roman rule. Many thought the Messiah would come soon. Mary probably heard the Messiah talked about everywhere she went.

Most of all, the Jews did not want to be forced to worship Roman gods. Mary and her family were no different. They longed for deliverance from these harsh Roman rules. They were looking for the Messiah to come and set them free just like everyone in their Jewish community.

DID YOU KNOW?

The Bible is made up of two sections: The Old Testament and the New Testament. These are also known as Scriptures. The Old Testament tells the history and beliefs of the Jews before Jesus was born. The Old Testament is the holy book of faith for the Jews. It has the Ten Commandments and their laws for daily life. This is the Bible that Mary heard read in the synagogue.

The New Testament tells the history and beliefs of Jesus and his followers. The first four books of the New Testament are Matthew, Mark, Luke, and John. These are called the Gospels. The Gospels tell about the life and teachings of Jesus.

BIBLE HERO

Jacob—Jacob's father was Isaac. Isaac's father was Abraham. God changed Jacob's name to Israel. His twelve sons became the leaders of the twelve tribes of Israel.

ONE GOD

Abraham chose to worship one God. This was different from other nations at the time. They worshiped many gods. Abraham passed his faith down to his children. They became known as the Jews. The Jews worshiped one God. Deuteronomy 6:4 says, "Israel, listen to me. The Lord is our God. The Lord is the one and only God."[1]

THE BIRTH OF THE MESSIAH

The **prophet** Micah lived over 700 years before Mary was born. Micah said the Messiah would be born in Bethlehem. Micah 5:2 says, "The Lord says, 'Bethlehem, you might not be an important town in the nation of Judah. But out of you will come a ruler over Israel for me."[2]

DID YOU KNOW?

Many scholars trust the Bible as an accurate historical account. **Bible scholar** Charlie Campbell says that there are "thousands of finds that have led me and many others to conclude the authors of the Bible left us an historically reliable record of real people, places, and events."[3]

Prophet: Person who tells God's words to others
Bible scholar: People who are trained to study the Bible and its history

Chapter 2

ENGAGED TO BE MARRIED

When we first read about Mary in the Bible, she is already old enough to be **engaged** to be married. In Bible times, most girls were teenagers when they became engaged. It is very likely Mary was quite young. She might have been thirteen or fourteen.

This may seem strange to us today. But in Mary's day, it was not strange at all. This is because people often died young from diseases or accidents. So when a girl was old enough to have children, she was old enough to get married.

In Bible times, an engagement was taken seriously. Jewish law said an engagement could not be broken except by a **divorce**. After an engagement of about a

Engaged: To make a promise to marry someone
Divorce: To end a marriage by law

© MarinaMariya/Shutterstock

year, the couple would be officially married.

Mary was engaged to a man named Joseph. Joseph belonged to the tribe of Judah. His

> Mary was probably still a teenager when she was engaged to be married.

ancestor was King David but Joseph was not royalty, he was a poor **carpenter**.

Mary's family and Joseph's family probably made the arrangements for their engagement and marriage, unlike today's couples who make their own decisions about marriage. Joseph probably paid a "**bride price**" to Mary's family. Then Mary and Joseph were ready for their wedding day after a short wait.

Carpenter: Person who makes things out of wood
Bride price: Money a man paid as a promise to marry a woman

Many artists have painted pictures of the angel Gabriel speaking with Mary.

It was at this time, during their engagement, that something very special happened. Mary saw an **angel**. The angel's name was Gabriel. Mary felt afraid! She didn't know what to think.

Gabriel spoke to Mary. He said, "Do not be afraid, Mary. God is very pleased with you."[1]

Then the angel Gabriel gave an important message to Mary. He said, "You will become **pregnant** and give birth to a son. You must name him Jesus. He will be great and will be called the Son of the Most High God. The Lord God will make him a king like his father David of long ago. He will rule forever over his people, who came from Jacob's family. His **kingdom** will never end."[2]

Mary had grown up going to the synagogue. She had heard the Scriptures read aloud. She had heard everyone talking about the coming Messiah. And most likely, Mary realized the angel was talking about the Messiah. The Messiah was supposed to be a king like King David. He was supposed to rule forever over the Jews and be the **Son of God**.

But Mary felt upset at the angel's words. What did the Messiah have to do with her? She was just a young

Angel: A messenger of God
Pregnant: Having a baby
Kingdom: People or lands ruled by a king
Son of God: A title for Jesus (meaning he is the Messiah)

woman who lived in Nazareth. And she didn't know how she could get pregnant. She wasn't married yet!

© Lars Justinen/GoodSalt

King David was the second king who ruled Israel. Many Jews thought the Messiah would come as a king.

The angel answered Mary's questions. Gabriel said, "The **Holy Spirit** will come to you. The power of the Most High God will cover you. So the holy one that is born will be called the Son of God."[3]

The angel added one more thing to his message. He said, "Your **relative** Elizabeth is old. And even she is going to have a child. People thought she could not have children. But she has been pregnant for six months now. Nothing is impossible with God."[4]

Now Mary had something else to think about. Her relative Elizabeth was pregnant even though she was really too old to have a baby! Only God could make

Holy Spirit: The Spirit of God
Relative: Person in a family

something like that happen. Mary's faith was made stronger.

Mary told the angel, "I serve the Lord. May it happen to me just as you said it would."[5]

Then the angel disappeared.

DID YOU KNOW?

Angels are mighty warriors. They serve God. The angel Gabriel brought a message from God to Mary. He brought a message from God to Daniel too. Daniel lived 550 years before Mary. Gabriel also brought a special message to a man named Zechariah. Gabriel told Zechariah that he and his wife Elizabeth, Mary's cousin, would have a son named John.

BIBLE HEROES

David—David was Israel's most important king. King David made Jerusalem the capital of Israel. Scriptures said the Messiah would be a **descendant** of David.

Elizabeth—Elizabeth was a faithful believer in God. She was a relative of Mary's and the mother of John the Baptist.

Descendant: Person born of a certain family

EYEWITNESS ACCOUNT

Mary was an **eyewitness**. Mary didn't write a book about what she saw and knew about Jesus but Matthew and Luke did. And Mary knew Matthew and other friends of Jesus.

Most likely Mary told the things she knew to friends of Jesus. Then they told the news to others. Luke says in the Gospel of Luke 1:2, "Reports of these things were handed down to us. There were people who saw these things for themselves from the beginning and then passed the word on."[6]

Eyewitness: Person who saw something actually happen

Chapter 3

BIRTH OF THE FIRSTBORN SON

The Bible tells us that Mary hurried to Elizabeth's house as soon as the angel left. Elizabeth lived many miles to the south of Nazareth. Her village was in the region of Judea. In those days, there was a good system of roads. Mary would have traveled on some of these roads to reach the house of her relative.

Elizabeth lived closer to Jerusalem than Mary. That was probably because her husband Zechariah worked at the temple in Jerusalem as a priest who helped serve.

When Mary got to Elizabeth's house, an amazing thing happened. Elizabeth heard Mary's greeting. At this, the baby inside Elizabeth jumped. Then Elizabeth cried out to Mary, "God has blessed you more than other women. And blessed is the child you will have!"[1] Mary was so happy she sang a song.

Mary stayed with her relative for three months,

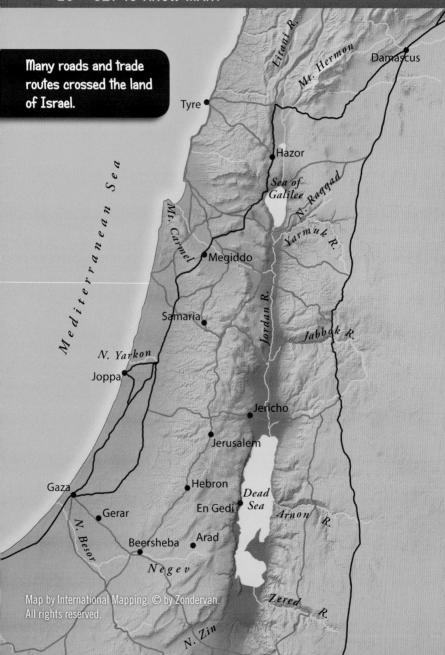

Many roads and trade routes crossed the land of Israel.

Damascus

Mt. Hermon

Litani R.

Tyre

Hazor

Sea of Galilee

N. Raqqad

Mediterranean Sea

Mt. Carmel

Megiddo

Yarmuk R.

Samaria

Jordan R.

Jabbok R.

N. Yarkon

Joppa

Jericho

Jerusalem

Gaza

Hebron

Dead Sea

En Gedi

Arnon R.

Gerar

N. Besor

Beersheba

Arad

Negev

Zered R.

N. Zin

until it was time for Elizabeth to have her baby. Elizabeth's baby was named John. He grew up to become John the Baptist.

Mary returned home to Nazareth after John was born. By now people knew she was pregnant. Joseph knew too. But he did not yet know that God was the Father of this special child. Joseph thought Mary had done something wrong. He decided to divorce her. This was the proper way to end an engagement. But an angel then appeared to Joseph too! The angel came to Joseph while he was sleeping.

The angel said, "Joseph, son of David, don't be afraid to take Mary home as your wife. The baby inside her is from the Holy Spirit. She is going to have a son. You must give him the name Jesus. That is because he will save his people from their sins."[2]

Now Joseph knew what Mary knew. He would obey the angel and take Mary as his wife. Soon the day for their wedding arrived. Mary moved out of her family's house and into Joseph's house.

It was at this same time that Caesar Augustus ordered a census. Everyone had to travel to the original hometown of his ancestors to be counted. Joseph's ancestor was King David. King David had been born in Bethlehem, so Joseph and Mary had to travel from

Nazareth to Bethlehem. That's where the Roman soldiers would count them and put their names on a list.

Mary and Joseph went where they were told to go. It was crowded when they reached Bethlehem. It seemed like almost everyone in the whole Roman Empire was traveling because of the order from Rome. Joseph tried to find a room for them to stay in, but the city was too crowded. The inns were full. Mary and Joseph finally found a place to stay, in the same place some animals lived.

Caesar Augustus

There were many caves in the village of Bethlehem. People often kept their animals in these caves. Some Bible scholars think that Mary and Joseph might have stayed in one.

© Marie-Lan Nguyen/Wikimedia Commons, CC BY 2.5

By then, it was time for Mary's baby to be born. It was the middle of the night. Usually a woman called a **midwife** helped with a baby's birth. But Joseph might

Midwife: Someone who helps a woman have a baby

have had to help Mary, we are not sure.

After baby Jesus was born, Mary probably washed him. Then she rubbed his skin with salt, and wrapped baby Jesus with strips of clean cloth. These were called **swaddling clothes**.

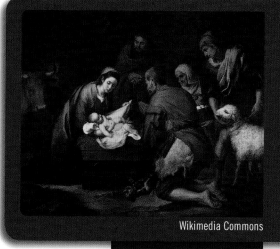

Wikimedia Commons

The shepherds came to Bethlehem to find Jesus.

Then she put baby Jesus in the manger. It was filled with sweet-smelling hay and was a soft and safe crib for the new little baby to sleep in.

Joseph's new family had surprise visitors that night! A group of shepherds arrived. They were very excited and had an amazing story to tell. The shepherds told how they had seen angels appear in the night sky. The angels were singing and praising God! One of the angels told

Swaddling clothes: Cloths to wrap around a baby like a blanket

the shepherds to go to Bethlehem. He said a **Savior** had been born there that night who was **Christ** the Lord.

The angel told the shepherds to look for a baby wrapped in strips of cloth. He also said the baby would be lying in a manger. The shepherds found baby Jesus with Mary and Joseph exactly as the angels had said.

Then the shepherds went back to their fields. On the way they told everyone what they had seen and heard. People were amazed at their words.

Mary was amazed too. It was hard for her to understand everything that was going on. It was hard for her to understand all of God's plan. But the Bible tells us that "Mary kept all these things like a secret treasure in her heart. She thought about them over and over."[3]

EYEWITNESS ACCOUNT

Josephus was an historian. He lived around the same time Mary did. He wrote about the history of the Jews and of Rome. He tells how King Herod the Great used 1,000 priests to build the temple in Jerusalem. Josephus said that King Herod "had some of them taught the arts of stone-cutters, and others of carpenters, and then began to build."[4]

Savior: The One who saves people

Christ: Greek word meaning "Messiah"

MARY'S SONG

The Bible records Mary's song in Luke 1:46–55.[5]

"My soul gives glory to the Lord.

My spirit delights in God my Savior.

He has taken note of me

even though I am not important.

From now on all people will call me blessed.

The Mighty One has done great things for me.

His name is holy."

BIBLE HERO

John the Baptist—John the Baptist called people to turn away from sin and turn to God. He baptized them in the Jordan River. He even baptized Jesus, although Jesus never sinned!

DID YOU KNOW?

Two main roads came together in Bethlehem. Tired travelers would often stop and look for an inn where they could stop and rest.

Chapter 4

THE NEWBORN KING

It was a very busy time for Mary and Joseph. Taking care of a new baby is a lot of work and they were far away from home.

Mary and Joseph also had a lot of important things to do. Jewish law said that every baby boy must be **circumcised**. Jesus was circumcised when he was eight days old in a special ceremony. During this ceremony they announced Jesus' name. Usually the first son in a family was named the same as the father but he was a very special baby. The angel had told Mary and Joseph to name him Jesus which means, "God saves."

Jewish law also said a firstborn son was holy to the Lord. His parents had to take him to a priest for

 Circumcised: A surgery sometimes given to baby boys

blessing. So Mary and Joseph had to travel again. This time they did not have to go very far. They went from Bethlehem to the big city of Jerusalem. They took baby Jesus to the temple there. Jesus was 40 days old.

According to tradition, some parents **sacrificed** a lamb at the temple when they took their first son there. But Mary and Joseph were very poor. They sacrificed two doves instead to follow the laws in the Scriptures.

Wikimedia Commons

King Herod the Great started rebuilding the temple in 20 BC. It was finished in 64 AD.

Something surprising happened at the temple while the new family was there. Two holy people were there. One was an old man named Simeon. The other was a very old woman

Sacrificed: Gave a special gift to God, such as an animal or grain

named Anna. Both were waiting for the coming of the Messiah, the Christ.

Simeon held the baby Jesus in his arms. He said a **blessing** over Jesus and his parents. He also told Mary that a sword would wound her soul. He said that God had sent Jesus to the people of Israel. Simeon believed Jesus was the Christ.

Then Anna saw Jesus too. She was 84 years old. She said a prayer of thanks to God. Then she told everyone she saw

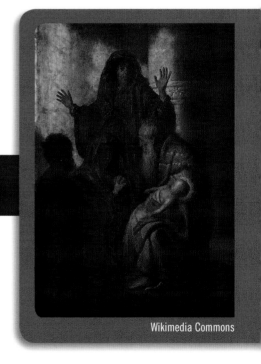

Simeon and Anna see Jesus at the temple.

about Jesus. Like her, they were looking for Christ to come, and it was good news.

Joseph and Mary

Wikimedia Commons

Blessing: A good thing from God

were amazed at the special attention given to Jesus. First the angels. Then the shepherds. Now this. Everyone was saying Jesus was the Christ.

Then later, another group of visitors came to see Jesus. Mary and Joseph were living in a house in Bethlehem. Jesus was old enough to be called a child. One day a group of rich men arrived. They looked like kings! They were **wise men** who lived in the land east of Bethlehem. These wise men had seen a special star. It led them to the house where Mary and Joseph were living.

When the wise men saw Jesus, they **bowed** down. They worshiped Jesus. Then they gave him gifts of incense, gold, and myrrh. They called Jesus, "the King of the Jews."[1]

After the wise men left to go home, Joseph had another dream. God spoke to Joseph in the dream.

God said, "Get up! Take the child and his mother and escape to Egypt. Stay there until I tell you to come back. Herod is going to search for the child. He wants to kill him."[2]

Wise Men: Scholars from Persia who gave gifts to Jesus

Bowed: Bent, usually at the waist, as a sign of worship or respect

The Journeys of Mary and Joseph

Journey of Mary and Joseph
from Nazareth to Bethlehem
for Jesus' birth

Jesus' family flees to Egypt
from Bethlehem out of fear that
Herod would kill Jesus

Return of Mary, Joseph, and
Jesus from Egypt on their way
to Nazareth

GALILEE

Capernaum

Sea of
Galilee

Nazareth

Jordan R.

Mediterranean Sea

SAMARIA

Antipatris

Shechem

PHILISTIA

JUDEA

Jerusalem

Bethlehem

Gaza

Hebron

Dead
Sea

Pelusium

To Egypt

Destination in
Egypt is unknown

0   40 km.

0   40 miles

Joseph got up in the middle of the night. He took
Mary and Jesus to Egypt as fast as he could.

Why did they leave so quickly? King Herod the
Great had heard about the Wise Men's visit. He had
talked with them himself and heard they were looking

for the newborn King of the Jews. He had found out this baby had been born in Bethlehem. King Herod was **paranoid**. He did not want anyone else to be king. So he made plans to kill Jesus. King Herod gave an order to kill every boy child in Bethlehem who was two years old or younger. Roman soldiers marched into Bethlehem. They followed King Herod's order. It was time of great **mourning** for many families.

But King Herod did not kill Jesus. Jesus was safe in Egypt with Mary and Joseph.

A short time after that, in 4 BC, King Herod died. God gave Joseph another dream. He told Joseph that King Herod was dead. So Mary,

Wikimedia Commons

King Herod the Great was buried here at Herodium. This palace was south of Jerusalem.

Joseph, and Jesus traveled back toward

Paranoid: Worry that everyone is trying to hurt you

Mourning: Feeling very sad, usually because of a death

Israel. Then Joseph got more news. King Herod's son Archelaus was ruling over Judea now. He was an evil king too.

So Mary and Joseph did not go back to Bethlehem in Judea. They traveled north to Galilee where a different son of Herod's was king. They moved back home to Nazareth.

EYEWITNESS ACCOUNT

The wise men went to see Herod at his magnificent palace in Jerusalem. Josephus said, Herod "also built himself a palace in the Upper city, containing two very large and most beautiful apartments."[3]

OUT OF EGYPT

The Scriptures said the Messiah would travel out of Egypt. Hosea 11:1 says, "I chose to bring my son out of Egypt."

DID YOU KNOW?

Archelaus was one of Herod the Great's sons. He ruled over Judea and Samaria. He was such an evil king that Rome took his power away. Some years later, Pilate became governor of Judea.

Chapter 5

THE TOWN OF NAZARETH

Mary, Joseph, and Jesus lived in the town of Nazareth. About twenty thousand people lived there at this time.

The Sea of Galilee was to the east of Nazareth. It was about fourteen miles away. Mary and Joseph could get there in one day on a donkey. They would see many fishermen and their boats along the shores.

An important city was nearby. The city of Sepphoris was just three miles away. It was the capital and largest city of Galilee, with possibly over fifty thousand people living there.

Herod Antipas was king of this area. He was a son of Herod the Great. Just like his father, he was known for his building projects. There were big buildings all

JACK GUEZ/AFP/Getty Images

Mary and Joseph lived in Nazareth. This is where Jesus grew up. In 2009, archaeologists found a home built about the time of Jesus.

over Sepphoris. The **theater** was the most famous of all.

Mary and Joseph lived near the capital of Roman rule in Galilee. The roads were busy with traffic. They probably saw traders with their **caravans** of camels and donkeys loaded with things to sell almost daily.

The **marketplace** in Nazareth had things Mary and Joseph would have had to buy for their family. When Mary shopped at the marketplace there were different coins she might have used. Some coins were Roman, some were **Greek**, and some were Jewish.

Theater: A place where people watched special events

Caravans: Groups of people who traveled together to stay safe

Marketplace: A place to buy and sell things, often outside

Greek: From the country of Greece, also the language the New Testament was written in

Mary had to be careful on market day. Often, traders tried to cheat their customers! Sometimes things were weighed on small **scales**. Other things were measured in pots or baskets. Short lengths of

The marketplace was a busy place in Israel.

© ChameleonsEye/Shutterstock

cloth or rope were measured based on the size of a hand. Market day could be any day of the week except the **Sabbath**. The Sabbath was a holy day of rest for

Scale: Tool used to weigh things

Sabbath: A special day of rest from Friday night to Saturday night

the Jews. Nobody could work on the Sabbath, which was from sundown Friday to sundown Saturday.

Mary probably bought fruits, vegetables, and olive oil from the marketplace. Local farmers sold these. Other products such as jewelry, **papyrus**, and some special foods were brought from places all over the Roman Empire such as Egypt, Babylonia, and Greece.

Local crafters sold their goods on market day too. Most likely, Mary bought clothes for the family there. These were woven on large **looms**. She probably bought long inner robes made of one piece of cloth. These were for Joseph, Jesus, and her other sons. She bought outer **tunics** for them to wear over that and similar clothes for herself and her daughters.

While Mary did the traditional jobs that belong to the woman of the house, Joseph and Jesus worked to make a living for the family. Joseph was a carpenter. Carpenters made wooden furniture for the community, such as stools and chairs. They also may have made tools, door posts, and wheels from wood and sold them at the marketplace.

Looms: Machines for making cloth out of yarn

Tunics: Long shirts

DID YOU KNOW?

Mary probably used different kinds of coins.

ROMAN COINS:

Quadran: This bronze coin is the smallest Roman coin.

As: Four quadrans equaled one bronze as.

Denarius: Sixteen as coins equaled one silver denarius.

GREEK COINS:

Drachma: One Roman denarius equaled one silver drachma.

Didrachma: Two drachmas equaled one silver didrachma.

Tetradrachma: Four drachmas equaled one silver tetradrachma.

Mina: 100 drachmas equaled one silver mina.

JEWISH COIN:

Lepton: This coin was smaller than the Roman quadran and equal to half its amount

Denarius

Tetradrachma

Lepton

DID YOU KNOW?

After King Herod died, his kingdom was divided amongst his three sons.

EYEWITNESS ACCOUNT

Josephus said Sepphoris "was the largest city of Galilee, and built in a place by nature very strong."[1]

Chapter 6

MARY AND JOSEPH'S HOME

Most likely Mary and Joseph lived in a very simple home in Nazareth. (According to some **traditions**, they may even have lived in a cave.) Some poor people in that area lived in caves at that time. Others lived in small houses. These simple homes had one room. Everyone lived, ate, and slept in one area of the room. If they were too poor to own a stable, their sheep or donkey often slept inside too. This protected the animals from hungry lions or bears.

Homes found in this area often had a **platform** on one part of the floor. It was raised up off the ground. This is where the family lived. Next to that was a dirt

Tradition: Ideas, words, or customs handed down from person to person usually in a family

Platform: An area built higher than another area

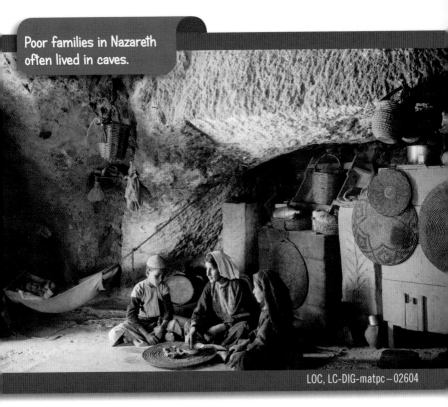

Poor families in Nazareth often lived in caves.

LOC, LC-DIG-matpc—02604

floor where the animals stayed. There was a manger to hold the animals' food on the dirt floor as well.

The walls of some houses were made of stone. Sometimes they were built with bricks made from mud and straw. The walls were often whitewashed. There might be one or two small windows and a door.

In many homes, the roof was flat. Usually there were stairs outside to climb up to the roof. Families often slept on the roof in the summer when it was hot.

Mary and Joseph's house probably didn't have much furniture. In Bible times, people slept on mats. Mary, Joseph, Jesus, and the other children probably slept side by side on their mats. Then they rolled them up in the morning and stacked the mats next to a wall.

Their table was probably an animal skin on the floor. Mary and her family sat on the floor or on mats to eat. Baskets and clay pots held food and water.

Mary probably cooked outside in the summer. This helped keep the house cool. In the winter, she would have built a fire on the floor just inside the door. Bread was baked on upside-down pots over the fire or in a small oven. Leeks, lentils, and beans were cooked in a pot to make soup. Grasshoppers were fried in olive oil. Locusts could be boiled in water or mixed with honey and flour to make biscuits. Goat's milk was made into yogurt, butter, and cheese. Poor families usually did not eat much meat except fish.

When her children were sick, Mary took care of them herself. In Bible times, honey was spread on cuts or wounds. Figs were cooked into a paste and put on **boils**, a swelling and infected part of the skin. Olive oil

Boils: An infected part of the skin

was rubbed into the hair of someone who was sick. Garlic was often used to help cure a toothache.

Summers were hot and dry in Nazareth. Figs, dates, grapes, and other fruits were **harvested** at the end of hot summers. Mary could then buy these at the marketplace.

Figs

© alisafarov/Shutterstock

Winter was the rainy season. It lasted from October through April. Days were cooler in the winter. The fields around Nazareth grew barley and wheat. Sheep, donkeys, and cows grazed on the green grass that grew thanks to the rain.

Mary might wash clothes in the streams that formed when it rained hard or with water she got from the village well. Soap was made from animal fat mixed with ashes from plants.

When visitors came to Mary and Joseph's home, their feet were washed. Perfumed oil would be poured

Harvested: Picked fruits, vegetables, or grains from the fields

Grass was more abundant after the rainy season.

www.HolyLandPhotos.org

on their hair. These were polite traditional things to do to welcome guests. That's because it was hot and dusty in this area of the world and travelers got dirty walking from place to place or riding on donkeys.

People took baths in rivers or with water from the well. The Romans that were living in the area built public **bathhouses**. The Jewish people could take

Bathhouses: Buildings with pools where people could take a bath

baths there too. Jewish law said it was important to keep clean. This showed that people were holy before God.

FROM NAZARETH

Unknown prophets said the Messiah would live in Nazareth. Matthew 2:23 says, "So what the prophets had said about Jesus came true. They had said, 'He will be called a Nazarene.'"[1]

EYEWITNESS ACCOUNT

An ancient letter was written that described the many fruits and crops grown in Israel. The letter said, "For the land is thickly planted with multitudes of olive trees, with crops of corn and pulse, with vines too, and there is abundance of honey. Other kinds of fruit trees and dates do not count compared with these."[2]

DID YOU KNOW?

In Jewish homes, fathers taught their trade to their sons. Jesus and his brothers grew up learning how to be a carpenter like Joseph.

Chapter 7

SHARING FAITH WITH HER FAMILY

Mary had an important **role** as a wife and mother. Mary taught many important things to Jesus and her other children. She passed down her Jewish **heritage** to them. She raised them to be faithful and obedient to God.

The Bible tells us that Jesus had at least four brothers. Their names were James, Joseph, Simon, and Judas (or Jude). Jesus had sisters too. Mary and Joseph had a large family which certainly kept Mary very busy working every day.

Mary had cooking and day-to-day household **chores**. She had other important duties as well. It was her job to teach her daughters at home. In Bible times,

Role: What a person does
Heritage: A special custom or item handed down in a family
Chores: Jobs to do

girls did not go to school so Mary would have taught her daughters how to cook and take care of the house. She would also have taught them about the Scriptures and the Jewish faith.

Jesus may have learned to write on a tablet such as this school child's limestone tablet found in Israel.

© 1995 by Phoenix Data Systems

Most Jewish families sent their sons to school. They went to the synagogue. Mary and Joseph probably sent Jesus and his brothers each day. Their teachers taught them the Scriptures and the Jewish laws.

There were many important laws for Mary's family to follow. Many of these laws were about the Sabbath—the seventh day of the week. The Sabbath started on Friday at sundown and lasted until Saturday at sunset.

Friday was a very busy day for Mary and the other women. Mary had to clean the house, get water from the well, and cook extra food. The water and food had to last two days. This was because people could not work on the Sabbath.

On Friday, Mary also had to make sure the children were clean. Then the family ate the Sabbath meal together after sunset.

When Mary and her family got up on Saturday morning they went to the synagogue. Every town and village in Israel had a synagogue, usually built on a small hill. Mary sat with her daughters and younger sons. They would be in a separate part of the synagogue than the men, and they sat behind a screen.

Z. Radovan/www.BibleLandPictures.com

The scrolls of the Old Testament were kept in a special box called an ark. The first five books of the Old Testament are called the Torah. These Scriptures are also known as the Law of Moses.

Torah: The Jewish holy book of faith; the first five books in the Bible

Law of Moses: The first five books in the Bible that have the Ten Commandments

The men sat in the main part of the synagogue. Boys thirteen years old and older sat with the men on benches or mats and faced the front. The front of the synagogue was where the Scriptures were kept. The Old Testament was written on scrolls. These scrolls were kept in a cabinet or box called an **ark**.

Synagogue leaders read from the scrolls. Men from the community also took turns. Joseph surely took his turn as did Jesus and his brothers when they were old enough. After reading Scriptures aloud, the men **discussed** what was read. Important lessons were taught about the Scriptures by teachers called rabbis. After the reading, Mary and her family went back home and rested until sunset. Then the Sabbath was over.

At different times, according to Jewish law, Mary and Joseph were required to make sacrifices to God.

Dead Sea Scrolls of the book of Leviticus.

Z. Radovan/www.BibleLandPictures.com

Ark: A special box that held the scrolls at a synagogue

Discussed: Talked about

The Scriptures gave special rules for sacrifices. These sacrifices had special meaning. Some were a way of giving thanks to God and others were a way of asking God to **forgive** them for sins.

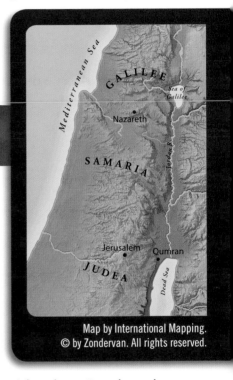

The Dead Sea Scrolls were found in caves in Qumran.

The Scriptures taught there must be a punishment for sins. When people felt sorry for their sins, they could offer a sacrifice. This had to be a dove, lamb, goat, or cow. The animal had to be perfect. It could not be sick or hurt. People took their animal to the priest to be sacrificed as a sign they felt sorry for their sins. The priest sprinkled the animal's blood on the **altar**. This was a sign that the blood

Map by International Mapping.
© by Zondervan. All rights reserved.

Forgive: To erase the record of sins

Altar: A table where sacrifices were offered

washed away their sins. After the sacrifice they were forgiven and did not have to be punished for their sins. They were made right with God.

THE SABBATH

In Exodus 20:8–10, the fourth of the Ten Commandments says, "Remember to keep the Sabbath day holy. Do all of your work in six days. But the seventh day is a Sabbath in honor of the Lord your God. Do not do any work on that day."[1]

DID YOU KNOW?

In Jewish tradition, a new day didn't start in the morning. A new day started at sunset. It lasted until sunset on the next day.

SACRIFICE FOR SIN

Old Testament law taught that people must bring a perfect animal to the priest to be sacrificed for their sins. Leviticus 4:31 says, "When the priest burns the offering, he will pay for the sin of that person. And he will be forgiven."[2]

Chapter 8

HOLIDAYS ARE HOLY DAYS

Jewish holidays were important to Mary and her family. The holidays they celebrated held deep meaning in their faith.

There were seven major Jewish holidays. They were called feasts and included Passover, **Unleavened** Bread, Firstfruits, Pentecost, Trumpets, Atonement, and Booths. Two other main holidays that were celebrated were Hanukkah and Purim.

Scriptures gave rules on how to celebrate these feasts. Mary and her family were careful to follow these rules.

Three of the feasts were **Pilgrim Feasts**. This meant

Unleavened Bread: Flat bread made without yeast so it doesn't rise

Pilgrim Feasts: Special days Jews had to travel to Jerusalem to celebrate

the Jews were required to travel to Jerusalem each year to celebrate Passover, Pentecost, and Booths.

© Mazor/www.istockphoto.com

The Feast of Trumpets begins with the blowing of the .

The Bible tells us that "every year Jesus' parents and the whole family went to Jerusalem for the Passover Feast. When he was twelve years old, they went up to the Feast as usual."[1] They traveled in large groups with relatives and friends. The roads to Jerusalem were very crowded because people traveled from all over the Roman Empire to celebrate.

The average **population** during Jesus' time in Jerusalem was about 30,000 people. Scholars think Jerusalem grew to between 100,000 and 300,000 during these Pilgrim Feasts. Mary and her family probably camped near the city. Large groups camped in the fields.

Shofar: a trumpet made from an animal's horn

Population: The number of people living in a place

The year Jesus was twelve, Mary and Joseph went to the temple as usual. Mary and her daughters waited in one area. Joseph took Jesus and his other sons to the priest. They presented their Passover lamb to be sacrificed. This was for the forgiveness of their sins. Blood from the lamb was sprinkled on the altar. This was to show that God had forgiven their sins. Finally, the meat of the lamb was given back to Joseph. Mary and Joseph then returned to their campsite. They gathered with relatives and **roasted** the lamb. Then they ate it together. This was the Passover meal.

The Passover meal was a special time for families. Mary and Joseph would tell their children about the history of the Jews. They told how the Jews had been slaves in Egypt over 1,000 years earlier. But God sent Moses to lead them out of Egypt and set them free.

Mary and Joseph talked about the Messiah. The Scriptures promised that God would one day send the Messiah to Israel. He would come and set them free.

Many Jews at this time hoped the Messiah would **overthrow** the Roman Empire. They hoped he would

---

Roasted: Cooked over a fire

Overthrow: To take power away from a government

rule over Israel. After all, this was the land God had promised them.

The next day was another feast. It was the Feast of Unleavened Bread. Mary and Joseph celebrated this feast in Jerusalem that year as well. During this feast, no bread made with **yeast** could be baked or eaten, only unleavened bread. This was to remind them of Moses leading the Jews out of Egypt. They had been forced to leave very quickly. There was no time for bread to rise. So for their final meal in Egypt the Jews had to eat unleavened, or flat, bread.

Unleavened bread is eaten during the Passover meal.

© picturepartners/Shutterstock

The Feast of Firstfruits came next. This celebrated the start of the spring barley harvest. Mary and Joseph would give a special offering of grain. This was a special time of joy and giving thanks to God for Mary and her family. They spent the days with crowds of people at

Yeast: Small plant material put in bread to make it rise

the temple. They enjoyed camping with family and friends. But finally, the holidays came to an end. It was time to go home.

Mary and Joseph packed up their things. They traveled on the road toward home. They did not see Jesus but they were not worried. They thought he was walking with their relatives and friends.

That night, they still had not seen Jesus. So Mary and Joseph looked for him. Nobody in their group had seen him! Now Mary and Joseph were worried. Where could Jesus be?

Mary and Joseph turned around. They went back to Jerusalem and looked for him everywhere. "After three days they found Jesus in the temple courtyard. He was sitting with the teachers listening to them and asking questions."[2] People in the crowds were amazed by Jesus. He understood so much! He answered the teachers so well.

Mary said, "Son, why have you treated us like this? Your father and I have been worried about you. We have been looking for you everywhere."[3]

"Why were you looking for me?" Jesus asked. "Didn't you know I had to be in my Father's house?"[4]

Mary and Joseph didn't know what Jesus was talking about. But they took Jesus with them and headed home.

Here at the temple, Jesus talked about the Scriptures with the priests and Jewish leaders when he was twelve.

Superstock/Getty Images

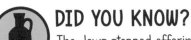

DID YOU KNOW?

The Jews stopped offering temple sacrifices in 70 AD. This was when Rome destroyed the temple in Jerusalem. However, some Jews in Samaria still sacrifice the Passover lamb today.

EYEWITNESS ACCOUNTS

Josephus wrote about some of the Jewish feasts. He said, "And indeed, at the feast of Unleavened Bread, which was now at hand, and is by the Jews called the Passover, and used to be celebrated with a great number of sacrifices, an innumerable multitude of the people came out of the country to worship."[5]

Josephus said, "That feast, which was observed after seven weeks, and which the Jews called Pentecost, (i.e. the 50th day) was at hand, its name being taken from the number of the days [after the Passover]."[6]

SEVEN FEASTS

In Leviticus 23, the Bible lists seven feasts the Jews were commanded to honor.

Passover: Celebrates when God delivered the Jews from the tenth plague

Unleavened Bread: Celebrates when Moses led the Jews out of Egypt

Firstfruits: Celebrates the start of the spring barley harvest

Pentecost (or Weeks): Celebrates the end of harvest and when God gave the Ten Commandments to his people

Feast of Trumpets (or Rosh Hashanah): Holy day announced with trumpet blasts

Day of Atonement (or Yom Kippur): Day when sin is paid for

Booths: Celebrates how God was with Moses and the Jews in the wilderness

Chapter 9

LIFE AND DEATH

Mary and Joseph returned to Nazareth. The Bible says in Luke 2:51 that Jesus "went back to Nazareth with them, and he obeyed them."[1]

Mary thought about what had happened. She remembered the amazing things that happened when Jesus was born. The Bible says that Mary "kept all these things like a secret treasure in her heart."[2]

In the years after that, Jesus grew up like a normal child of the time. So did Mary's other children. The New Testament mentions some of their names. However, there is no mention of Joseph in the Bible after that Passover. Perhaps Joseph died after that time.

When a family member died, the Jews followed special **customs**. Since Joseph was older than Mary, perhaps he died while Jesus was still growing up. In that case, Joseph's body would have been washed with perfume, spices, and oil. Then his body would have been wrapped in strips of white cloth. According to custom, Joseph's body then had to be buried the very same day he died.

Perfume and oil were kept in alabaster jars such as these.

© by Zondervan

Mary would have had a funeral for Joseph. His body would be put on a **stretcher**. Family members then carried the stretcher to the grave. People would have followed along in a **procession**.

In those days, people were often buried in tombs. These were rooms cut in rocks or caves. There were shelves in the tombs. Joseph's body would have been put on one of them. A large rock was put over the entrance to the tomb to keep thieves and wild animals away.

Customs: Common actions of people who live in the same area

Stretcher: A frame to help carry someone

Alabaster: a fine-grained mineral often used to make containers such as vases and jars

Procession: A kind of parade

After a long time, only Joseph's bones would be left. The bones would be put in a special box and put in another part of the tomb, then someone else's dead body could be put on the shelf.

After people died, their bones were put in special boxes such as this. This one belonged to Caiaphas, the high priest that put Jesus on trial.

Wikimedia Commons

In Bible times, many Jews believed that there was life after death. Most likely, Mary and her family did too. They believed Joseph was living in heaven with God.

Joseph's funeral would have been a sad time. But Mary celebrated happy times as well. The Bible tells us about one of these happy times. Mary went to a wedding in Cana.

A wedding day was a happy day for the whole community. Marriage was important. It had deep roots in the Jewish faith. The Bible says that God created marriage between a man and a woman and it was a holy event. Jewish weddings had special customs. Often, the father gave presents to the bride.

These could include servants or land. The **bridegroom** gave the bride presents too. He often gave her pretty jewelry and new clothes. Sometimes the bridegroom would give her a chain of silver coins to wear on her wedding day as jewelry.

The bridegroom put on special clothes. He went with his friends to the bride's house. The bride wore a special dress and **valuable** jewels. Often, she wore a **veil** to cover her face.

Sometimes the bride rode through the streets in a decorated chair. It was carried on the shoulders of the bridegroom's friends. The bride and groom and their friends went through the streets to the bridegroom's home like this.

People danced and sang. They played **tambourines** and other instruments. They ate delicious food. Weddings often lasted for a whole week.

We don't know if Mary stayed at the wedding in Cana the whole time. But we do know that Jesus went to the wedding too. So did some of his friends.

Bridegroom: Man who is getting married

Valuable: Very important or worth a lot of money

Veil: Thin piece of fabric that covers the face

Tambourines: Small musical instrument held in the hands and shaken

Everyone that could, celebrated the holiness of marriage and the joys of life.

In Bible times, the bride was carried in a special chair.

© DINODIA/age fotostock

BIBLE HERO

Joseph—Joseph was the legal guardian of Jesus on earth. Joseph was Mary's husband. He could trace his ancestors back to King David and on back to Adam and Eve.

DID YOU KNOW?

Common instruments played in Bible times included bells, cymbals, harps, flutes, tambourines, and trumpets made from animal horns.

THE SONG OF SONGS

The Song of Songs is a book in the Old Testament. It was part of the Bible Mary heard at the synagogue. It is a group of love songs that celebrates the joy and holiness of marriage. Song of Songs 3:11 says, "Look at King Solomon wearing his crown. His mother placed it on him. She did it on his wedding day. His heart was full of joy."[3]

Chapter 10

DEALING WITH THE MESSIAH

What was it like for Mary to have Jesus as a son? We do not know, but the Bible gives us some clues. Some of these clues are found in the Gospels. The Gospels tell about the life and teachings of Jesus. The Gospels are the books of Matthew, Mark, Luke, and John and make up part of the New Testament in the Bible.

John was one of the **twelve disciples**. Jesus had hand-picked this group of twelve men. Jesus was their teacher. John and the others were with Jesus for three years. During those three years, John was an eyewitness to many things Jesus did. So was Matthew. And even though Mark and Luke weren't eyewitnesses

 Twelve Disciples: A special group of Jesus' closest followers

to the events written about in the Gospels, they were friends with people who were.

The words of an eyewitness are very important. Many scholars agree that the Gospels are accurate, true, and historical accounts of the life and teachings of Jesus. For example, the Gospel of John tells about the wedding at Cana. John was certainly there at the wedding with Mary, Jesus, and the other disciples. The guests must have been at the wedding in Cana for awhile when they ran out of wine. This would have been very **embarrassing** for the families of the bride and groom.

For some reason, Mary wanted to help. Perhaps the wedding was for a relative of Mary's or for one of her close friends.

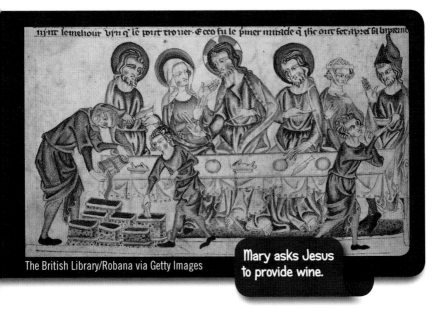

The British Library/Robana via Getty Images

Mary asks Jesus to provide wine.

So what did she do? John says she went to Jesus. She told him, "They have no more wine."[1]

Jesus answered his mother. "Dear woman, why do you bring me into this? My time has not yet come."[2]

But Mary still wanted to help. So she spoke with the servants. She said, "Do what he tells you."[3]

Near them were six very large stone water jars. Each one held twenty to thirty gallons of water. The water in these jars was used for a special purpose. The Jews washed with this water to make themselves holy. It was a tradition they had.

One large stone jar weighs almost 1,000 pounds.

Jesus spoke to the servants. He said, "Fill the jars with water."[4]

Todd Bolen/www.BiblePlaces.com

So the servants filled the jars up to the top with water.

Then Jesus told them to dip some of the water out. He said, "Take it to the person in charge of the dinner."[5]

Embarrassing: Something that makes a person feel strange or uncomfortable

The person tasted it. The water had turned into wine! It was a **miracle**. Only God could have done this.

After this happened, John tells us in his Gospel that Jesus' "disciples put their faith in him."[6]

How did Mary know to ask Jesus to do this? Had she seen Jesus do miracles at home, before he began his public ministry?

We don't know the answers to questions like this. But the Bible says that from then on, Jesus did many miracles. He fed 5,000 people with only five loaves of

Feeding the 5,000 is the only one of Jesus' miracles found in all four Gospels, other than when Jesus rose from the dead. This mosaic from Tabgha is the traditional location of the event.

Wikimedia Commons

Miracle: An amazing event that only God could have done

bread and two fish. He walked on water. He brought a dead girl back to life.

Jesus also told people he was the Messiah. He told them he was God. His words **shocked** many people. But some people believed what Jesus said. They believed he truly was the Messiah—God.

What did Mary think about all the things Jesus was doing and saying? Did she remember the special events that happened when he was born? Did she understand God's plan? Did she believe Jesus was the Messiah? Did she believe Jesus was God?

One day Mary went looking for Jesus. The Bible says, "Jesus' mother and brothers came to see him. But they could not get near him because of the crowd. Someone told him, 'Your mother and brothers are standing outside. They want to see you.'"[7]

The Gospel of Mark says that, "Jesus entered a house. Again a crowd gathered. It was so large that Jesus and his disciples were not even able to eat. His family heard about this. So they went to take charge of him. They said, 'He is out of his mind.'"[8] John says in

Shocked: Surprised

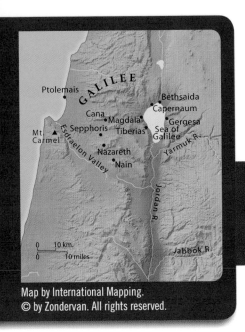

Ptolemais

GALILEE

Bethsaida
Capernaum
Cana
Magdala
Sepphoris   Tiberias   Sea of
Mt.   Galilee
Carmel

Esdraelon Valley

Nazareth

Nain

Yarmuk R.

Gergesa

Jordan R.

Jabbok R.

0   10 km.
0   10 miles

Map by International Mapping.
© by Zondervan. All rights reserved.

his Gospel that "even Jesus' own brothers did not believe in him."[9]

We don't know what Mary thought in her heart at this time.

> The early years of Jesus' ministry were in the cities of Galilee. The Bible notes that Mary was with him at some of these places.

But we can imagine it must have been a very hard time for her as a mother. What was her oldest son saying? What was he doing? Who did he think he was?

EYEWITNESS ACCOUNT

Peter was one of the twelve disciples. He witnessed a special time with Jesus. Jesus' clothes glowed like light and his face shone as the sun. In 2 Peter 1:16, Peter said, "We didn't make up stories when we told you about it. With our own eyes we saw him in all his majesty."[10]

ONE OF MANY MIRACLES

Jesus fed a large crowd with just five loaves of bread and two fish. Matthew 14:21–22 says, "The disciples picked up 12 baskets of leftover pieces. The number of men who ate was about 5,000. Women and children also ate."[11]

BIBLE HEROES

Matthew, Mark, Luke, and John—The Gospels were written by these four men:

Matthew was one of the twelve disciples. He was a tax collector and was also called Levi.

Mark left on a missionary trip with Paul and Barnabas, two early church leaders. Mark was a cousin of Barnabas and was also called John Mark.

Luke went on missionary journeys with Paul. He was a doctor.

John was one of the twelve disciples. He was a fisherman and the brother of James.

DID YOU KNOW?

In the Gospel of Luke and the Book of Acts, Luke gives a lot of details. "In his detailed accounts, he mentions thirty-two countries, fifty-four cities, nine islands, ports, the names and titles of priests and political leaders, deities that certain cities worshiped, weather patterns, particular shipping lanes, laws, and customs."[12] Many of these details have been proven true by different discoveries.

Chapter 11

AT THE CROSS

Jesus had been teaching and preaching for three years. He was thirty-three years old. It was spring and time for the Passover Feast again.

As she had done for so many years, Mary went with her friends and relatives to Jerusalem to celebrate Passover. Jesus was teaching in the temple there. Large crowds stood near him to listen. We don't know if Mary joined the crowds or not.

We do know that many people in the crowd were upset. The **chief priests** and Jewish leaders did not like how Jesus said he was the Messiah, the Christ. They did not like that Jesus said he was the Son of God. And they did not like how Jesus told people he was God.

Chief priests: A group of official Jewish leaders

This wall is the foundation of the western wall of the temple in Jerusalem. It is 2,000 years old and the only part of the temple still left standing today. It is called the **Western Wall**.

© mikhail/Shutterstock

Many people believed in him and this made the Jewish leaders upset and nervous.

The Jewish leaders planned to kill Jesus. They made arrangements with Judas, one of Jesus' disciples. One night, Judas led them to the **garden of Gethsemane**. Jesus was there with his other disciples, praying.

Jesus was arrested. He was put on trial before the **Sanhedrin**. This was the highest ranking group of Jewish leaders. They met in Jerusalem and made important decisions. They agreed Jesus should be killed. So Jesus was taken to see Pontius Pilate.

Pontius Pilate was the Roman governor of Judea.

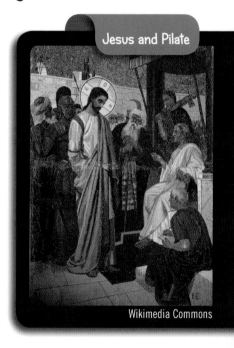

Jesus and Pilate

Wikimedia Commons

Foundation: The base of a building

Western Wall: A wall from Herod's Temple that still stands today

Garden of Gethsemane: A garden near Jerusalem

Sanhedrin: The group of highest-ranking Jewish leaders who met in Jerusalem and made important decisions

Pontius Pilate said Jesus was innocent. He told them, "I myself find no basis for a charge against him."[1]

But the Jews replied, "We have a law. That law says he must die. He claimed to be the Son of God."[2]

Finally, Pilate agreed. He "handed Jesus over to them to be nailed to a cross."[3]

The Roman soldiers took charge of Jesus. They led him outside the city of

Christ on the Cross between the Virgin and St. John, Spanish School/Musee des Beaux-Arts, Pau, France/Giraudon/The Bridgeman Art Library

Jesus chose John to take care of Mary when he was gone.

Jerusalem, to a place called The Skull.

The soldiers nailed Jesus to a wooden cross. Two other men, criminals, were also nailed on crosses. Jesus was in the middle.

The Bible says that "Jesus' mother stood near his cross."[4] Other women were there too. John, the disciple was also there. In the book of John, he tells how Jesus looked down from the cross at him and Mary.

Jesus said to Mary, "Dear woman, here is your son."[5] Then he said to John, "Here is your mother."[6]

This would have meant a lot to Mary. Jesus was her firstborn son. Jewish custom said the oldest son was supposed to take care of his mother. Since Jesus was dying, he chose John to take care of Mary when he was gone.

Finally, Jesus breathed his last breath. He said, "It is finished."[7] Then he bowed his head and died.

This day was certainly one of the saddest days in Mary's life. Mary saw her own son die. We don't know how long she stayed near the cross after Jesus died. We don't know when she left the place called the Skull. But the Bible says that after that day, Mary moved into John's house. John took care of her for the rest of her life.

NAILED TO THE CROSS

Psalm 22:16 says, "They have pierced my hands and my feet."[8] This is a Scripture about the Messiah. It was written 1,000 years before Jesus was born.

EYEWITNESS ACCOUNT

A writer named Lucian lived in the Roman Empire about 100 years after Jesus. He said, "The Christians, you know, worship a *man* to this day—the distinguished personage who introduced their novel rites, and was **crucified** on that account.[9]"

THE PASSOVER LAMB

Jesus was the Passover Lamb. He knew he was supposed to be sacrificed for the forgiveness of sins. It was part of God's plan. When the soldiers arrested him, Jesus told Peter, "Do you think I can't ask my Father for help? He would send an army of more than 70,000 angels right away. But then how would the Scriptures come true? They say it must happen in this way."[10]

Crucified: Killed on a cross

Chapter 12

A NEW BEGINNING

Jesus was buried in the tomb of a rich man named Joseph. The Bible says, "The women who had come with Jesus from Galilee followed Joseph. They saw the tomb and how Jesus' body was placed in it."[1]

Soon it was the Sabbath. The women rested just as the Scriptures commanded. Then some of the women from Galilee went back to the tomb. They took spices to put on Jesus' body. It was **dawn** on Sunday morning.

An amazing thing happened when they got to the tomb. Jesus' body was gone and angels were at the tomb. One angel said, "Don't be alarmed. You are looking for Jesus the Nazarene, who was crucified. But he has **risen**! He is not here! See the place where they

Dawn: Early morning

Risen: Came to life again after being dead

had put him. Go! Tell his disciples and Peter, 'He is going ahead of you into Galilee. There you will see him. It will be just as he told you.'"[2]

The women ran to tell everyone what had happened. Jesus was alive! This was happy news to Mary's ears. And then more reports came in. Jesus himself appeared to the believers.

Jesus met with different groups of his followers. He appeared to a crowd of 500 believers. He even met with his brother James. Jesus proved to his followers that he was alive again. He taught them the Old Testament Scriptures about the Messiah. He showed them how he **fulfilled** each one of those Scriptures. He told them he was God.

Forty days went by. Then Jesus went up to heaven in front of their eyes. He disappeared into the clouds. Then, angels appeared. The angels spoke to the disciples who were there. They told the believers to watch for Jesus. They said he would come back one day in the same way he left. This is called the Ascension.

Jesus had given special instructions to his followers while he was back for those 40 days. He told them to

Fulfilled: Completed or done

wait in Jerusalem. He said to wait for the Holy Spirit to come upon them. Jesus had explained the Holy Spirit would **anoint** them with power and this power would help them tell others about Jesus.

WikiPaintings

Mary waited in Jerusalem with the others. So did Jesus' brothers. They met together every day in an upstairs room and prayed.

Jesus ascends into heaven.

Mary finally understood. She remembered the special things that happened when Jesus was born—the angel's visit, the dreams Joseph had, the visits from the shepherds. She remembered the Passover when Jesus was twelve. She remembered the miracles Jesus had done. Now she knew all these things happened because Jesus was God. Mary believed Jesus was the Messiah, the Christ. So did Jesus' brothers.

Anoint: to choose, with God's intervention

Soon it was the day of Pentecost. Crowds of Jews had come to Jerusalem for the feast, just like always.

All of the believers were together in the upstairs room of a house. Most likely, Mary was there too. Suddenly everyone heard a loud noise. It came from heaven and sounded like a roaring wind.

They saw something that looked like fire. A flame settled on each person's head. Then everyone was filled with the Holy Spirit. Each person started to talk in a language they didn't know.

© Peter Zaharov/Shutterstock

According to tradition, it was in this room that Mary met with the disciples and the brothers of Jesus to pray. Although these events may have occurred in the vicinity, they could not have happened here—for this room was built 1,200 years after the events!

The crowds outside the house heard the noise. They came to see what was going on. They were very surprised. Everyone heard the believers speaking the message of God in their own language.

"What does this mean?"[3] they asked.

Peter was one of the twelve disciples.

He stood up and spoke. He gave a special message about Jesus. He explained that Jesus was the Passover Lamb and had been sacrificed to pay the punishment for sins.

Then Peter told the crowd that Jesus was the Messiah. Jesus was the one they were waiting for. He told them about the **resurrection**. He said that God raised Jesus from the dead. "We are all **witnesses** of this,"[4] Peter said.

Three thousand people in the crowd believed what Peter said. They chose to become followers of Jesus that day. The new church was born.

Years went by. The disciples Matthew and John wrote about the events they had experienced. Mary probably talked with them, telling them about what happened when Jesus was born and when he was growing up. They wrote about these things too.

In the Gospel of John, John wrote, "This is the disciple who gives witness to these things. He also wrote them down. We know that his witness is true."[5]

Mary may have told Jesus' story to others as well. These people who knew Mary probably talked with Mark and Luke. And they wrote about Jesus and his life too.

Resurrection: When Jesus rose from the dead and came alive again

Witnesses: People who see something happen

Eventually, their four books became the Gospels in the New Testament of the Bible—the books of Matthew, Mark, Luke, and John. Many scholars believe they are important historical documents—true accounts of

This is part of the Gospel of John. It was written about 125 AD. It is the oldest manuscript of the Gospels known today.

Centre for Public Christianity

people, places, and events.

Mary's story was now part of the Bible. The story of her son Jesus was too. People in future **generations** would learn about Jesus Christ the Messiah. They could choose to believe in Jesus too.

BIBLE HERO

Elijah—Elijah was a very important Old Testament prophet. He lived around 850 BC. His voice was heard saying God is the one true God.

Generations: People born around the same time

EYEWITNESS ACCOUNT

After Jesus rose from the dead, his brothers also believed he was the Messiah, the Christ. His brother James said, in James 1:1, "I serve God and the Lord Jesus Christ."[6]

His brother Jude said, in Jude 1:21, "The mercy of our Lord Jesus Christ will bring you eternal life."[7]

DID YOU KNOW?

Jesus lived, died, and came to life again at the perfect time in history. The Romans had built a great system of roads by then. This made it easy for the disciples to travel and the new church to spread all over the Roman Empire.

EYEWITNESS ACCOUNT

Josephus wrote about one of the **high priests** who was in power many years after Jesus. Josephus said, "He assembled the Sanhedrin of judges, and brought before them the brother of Jesus, who was called Christ, whose name was James, and some others, [or, some of his companions]; and when he had formed an accusation against them as breakers of the law, he delivered them to be **stoned**."[8]

High priest: The leader of all the priests

Stoned: Killed with stones

TIMELINE OF MARY
(dates are approximate)

Wikimedia Commons

20 BC
Mary is born

4 AD
Mary's son, Jesus, is born

© Nancy Bauer/Shutterstock

Wikimedia Commons

3 BC
Mary hears message
from angel

8 AD
Mary goes to Jerusalem
when Jesus is 12

WORLD HISTORY

31 BC–14 AD
Emperor Caesar Augustus

4 BC
Herod the
Great dies

14 AD–37 AD
Emperor Tiberius

Wikimedia Commons

Superstock

27 AD
Mary goes to wedding
in Cana

30 AD
Mary hears news that
Jesus is alive again

© Renata Sedmakova/Shutterstock

© Renata Sedmakova/Shutterstock

30 AD
Mary sees Jesus
die on the cross

30 AD
Mary meets with early
believers at Pentecost

25 AD
Western Han Dynasty
ends in China

26–36 AD
Pilate governs Judea

43 AD
London founded

GLOSSARY

Alabaster: A fine-grained mineral often used to make containers such as vases and jars

Altar: A table where sacrifices are burned

Ancestors: Parents, grandparents, and older people in a family

Angel: A messenger of God

Anoint: To pour out on someone

Ark: A special box that holds the scrolls at a synagogue

Baptized: A symbol of being washed clean from sin through faith in God

Bible scholar: People who are trained to study the Bible and its history

Blessed: Someone who gets good gifts from God

Blessing: A good thing from God

Bowed: Bent, usually at the waist, as a sign of worship or respect

Bridegroom: Man who is getting married

Bride price: Money a man paid as a promise to marry a woman

Capital: City where the leader rules

Caravans: Groups of people who traveled together to stay safe

Carpenter: Person who makes things out of wood

Census: An official count of people living in a certain place

Chief priests: A group of official Jewish leaders

Christ: Greek word meaning "Messiah"

Circumcised: A surgery sometimes given to baby boys

Cross: Two pieces of wood put together in the shape of a T that Romans used to kill people by hanging them on it

Crucified: Killed on a cross

Customs: Common actions of people who live in the same area

Dawn: Early morning

Descendant: Person born of a certain family

Discussed: Talked about

Divorce: To end a marriage by law

Embarrassing: Something that makes a person feel strange or uncomfortable

Emperor: The ruler over a group of countries

Engaged: To make a promise to marry someone

Eyewitness: Person who actually saw something happen

Forgive: To erase the record of sins

Foundation: The base of a building

Fulfilled: Completed or done

Garden of Gethsemane: A garden near Jerusalem

Generations: People born around the same time

Gospel: "Good news," each of the first four books of the New Testament

Greek: From the country of Greece, also the language the New Testament was written in

High priest: The leader of all the priests

Holiness: Being holy or special to God

Holy Spirit: The Spirit of God

Kingdom: People or lands ruled by a king

Law of Moses: The first five books in the Bible that have the Ten Commandments

Manger: Box that holds food for animals

Marketplace: A place to buy and sell things, often outside

Messiah: The promised Savior of the Jews

Midwife: Someone who helps a woman have a baby

Miracles: Amazing events that only God could have done

Missionary: Person who takes his faith to others

Mourning: Feeling very sad, usually because of a death

Nativity: The birth of Jesus

Overthrow: To take power away from a government

Papyrus: A kind of paper made from plants

Paranoid: Worry that everyone is trying to hurt you

Pilgrim Feasts: Feasts that Jews had to travel to Jerusalem to celebrate

Population: The number of people living in a place

Pregnant: Having a baby

Priest: Person who performs important ceremonies of faith

Procession: A kind of parade

Prophet: Person who tells God's words to others

Relative: Person in a family

Resurrection: When Jesus rose from the dead and came alive again

Risen: Came to life again after being dead

Roasted: Cooked over a fire

Sabbath: A special day of rest from Friday night to Saturday night

Sacrificed: Gave a special gift to God such as an animal or grain

Sanhedrin: The highest group of Jewish leaders who met in Jerusalem and made important decisions

Savior: The One who saves people from getting punished for their sins

Scale: Tool used to weigh things

Shocked: Surprised

Shofar: A trumpet made from an animal's horn

Sins: Bad things people think, say, or do

Son of God: A title for Jesus meaning he is the Messiah

Stable: Barn for animals

Stoned: Killed with stones

Stretcher: A frame to help carry someone

Swaddling clothes: Cloths to wrap around a baby like a blanket

Synagogue: Building where Jews meet for worship

Tambourines: Small musical instrument held in the hands and shaken

Ten Commandments: Ten holy laws given by God to the Jews

Theater: A place where people watched special events

Torah: The Jews' holy book of faith, the first five books in the Bible

Tribes: Different groups within the same family

Twelve Disciples: A special group of Jesus' closest followers

Unleavened Bread: Flat bread that didn't rise

Unrest: Unhappy people, often in regard to leadership

Valuable: Very important or worth a lot of money

Veil: Thin piece of fabric that covers the face

Wailing Wall: A wall from Herod's Temple that still stands today

Wise Men: Scholars from Persia who gave gifts to Jesus

Witnesses: People who see something happen

Yeast: Small plant material put in bread to make it rise

SELECTED BIBLIOGRAPHY

Alexander, David and Pat. *Zondervan Handbook to the Bible.* Grand Rapids, Michigan: Zondervan, 2002.

"Antiquities of the Jews," *The Works of Flavius Josephus*, December 21, 2013, http://www.sacred-texts.com/jud/josephus/index.htm.

Burge, Gary M. *Jesus and the Jewish Festivals.* Grand Rapids, Michigan: Zondervan, 2012.

Campbell, Charlie H. *Archaeological Evidence for the Bible: Exciting Discoveries Verifying Persons, Places and Events in the Bible.* Carlsbad, California: The Always Be Ready Apologetics Ministry, 2012.

Campbell, Charlie H. *One Minute Answers to Skeptics' Top Forty Questions.* United States: Aquintas Publishing, 2005.

Charles, R.H. Editor, *The Letter Of Aristeas.* Oxford: The Clarendon Press, 1913, as found on April 30, 2013 at "The Letter of Aristeas, 112," http://www.ccel.org/c/charles/otpseudepig/aristeas.htm.

Connelly, Douglas. *Amazing Discoveries that Unlock the Bible: A Visual Experience.* Grand Rapids, Michigan: Zondervan, 2008.

Free, Joseph P. and Howard F. Vos. *Archaeology and Bible History.* Grand Rapids, Michigan: Zondervan, 1992.

Gardner, Paul D. *New International Encyclopedia of Bible Characters.* Grand Rapids, Michigan: Zondervan, 1995.

Gower, Ralph. *The New Manners and Customs of Bible Times.* Chicago: Moody Press, 1987.

Hindson, Ed. *Bible Prophecy from A to Z*. Forest, Virginia: The King is Coming College, 2012.

House, H. Wayne. *Zondervan Charts: Chronological and Background Charts of the New Testament*. Grand Rapids: Michigan, 2009.

Matthews, Victor H. *Manners and Customs in the Bible*. Peabody, Massachusetts: Hendrickson Publishers, 1991.

Missler, Chuck. *Learn the Bible in 24 Hours*. Nashville: Thomas Nelson Publishers, 2002.

Rasmussen, Carl G. *Zondervan Atlas of the Bible*. Grand Rapids: Zondervan, 2010.

Silva, Moisé and J.D. Douglas and Merrill C. Tenney. *Zondervan Illustrated Bible Dictionary*. Grand Rapids, Michigan: Zondervan, 2011.

Strobel, Lee. *The Case for the Resurrection*. Grand Rapids, Michigan: Zondervan, 2009.

Tenney, Merrill C., General Editor. *The Zondervan Encyclopedia of the Bible, Volumes 1–5*. Grand Rapids, Michigan: Zondervan, 2009.

"The Death of Peregrine, 11," *Works of Lucian of Samosata*, May 6, 2013, http://sacred-texts.com/cla/luc/wl4/wl420.htm.

"The Wars of the Jews," *The Works of Flavius Josephus*, April 6, 2013, http://www.sacred-texts.com/jud/josephus/index.htm.

Throckmorton, Burton H. Jr. *Gospel Parallels: A Synopsis of the First Three Gospels*. Nashville: Thomas Nelson Publishers, 1979.

Vos, Howard F. *Nelson's New Illustrated Bible Manners & Customs*. Nashville: Thomas Nelson, 1999.

Walton, John H., Mark L. Strauss, and Ted Cooper Jr. *The Essential Bible Companion*. Grand Rapids, Michigan: Zondervan, 2006.

SOURCE NOTES

CHAPTER 1: A DAUGHTER IN THE HOUSE OF JACOB

1. Deuteronomy 6:4, NIrV

2. Micah 5:2, NIrV

3. Campbell, Charlie H. *Archaeological Evidence for the Bible: Exciting Discoveries Verifying Persons, Places and Events in the Bible.* Carlsbad, California: The Always Be Ready Apologetics Ministry, 2012, page 136.

CHAPTER 2: ENGAGED TO BE MARRIED

1. Luke 1:30, NIrV

2. Luke 1:31–33, NIrV

3. Luke 1:35, NIrV

4. Luke 1:36–37, NIrV

5. Luke 1:38, NIrV

6. Luke 1:2, NIrV

CHAPTER 3: BIRTH OF THE FIRSTBORN SON

1. Luke 1:42, NIrV

2. Matthew 1:20–21, NIrV

3. Luke 2:19, NIrV

4. "Antiquities of the Jews, 15.11.2," *The Works of Flavius Josephus*, April 29, 2013, http://www.sacred-texts.com/jud/josephus/ant–15.htm.

5. Luke 1:46–49, NIrV

CHAPTER 4: THE NEWBORN KING

1. Matthew 2:2, NIrV

2. Matthew 2: 13, NIrV

3. "The Wars of the Jews, 1.21.1," *The Works of Flavius Josephus*, April 30, 2013, http://www.sacred-texts.com/jud/josephus/war–1.htm.

CHAPTER 5: THE TOWN OF NAZARETH

1. "War of the Jews, 3.2.4," *The Works of Flavius Josephus*, April 30, 2013, http://www.sacred-texts.com/jud/josephus/war–3.htm.

CHAPTER 6: MARY AND JOSEPH'S HOME

1. Matthew 2:23, NIrV

2. Charles, R.H. Editor, *The Letter Of Aristeas*. Oxford: The Clarendon Press, 1913, as found on April 30, 2013 at "The Letter of Aristeas, 112," http://www.ccel.org/c/charles/otpseudepig/aristeas.htm.

CHAPTER 7: SHARING FAITH WITH HER FAMILY

1. Exodus 20:8–10, NIrV

2. Leviticus 4:31, NIrV

CHAPTER 8: HOLIDAYS ARE HOLY DAYS

1. Luke 2:41–42, NIrV

2. Luke 2:46, NIrV

3. Luke 2:48, NIrV

4. Luke 2:49, NIrV

5. "The Wars of the Jews, 2.1.3," *The Works of Flavius Josephus*, May 2, 2013, http://www.sacred-texts.com/jud/josephus/war–2.htm.

6. "The Wars of the Jews, 2.1.3," *The Works of Flavius Josephus*, May 2, 2013, http://www.sacred-texts.com/jud/josephus/war–2.htm.

CHAPTER 9: LIFE AND DEATH

1. Luke 2:51, NIrV

2. Luke 2:51, NIrV

3. Song of Songs 3:11, NIrV

CHAPTER 10: DEALING WITH THE MESSIAH

1. John 2:3, NIrV

2. John 2:4, NIrV

3. John 2:5, NIrV

4. John 2:7, NIrV

5. John 2:8, NIrV

6. John 2:11, NIrV

7. Luke 8:19–20, NIrV

8. Mark 3:20–21, NIrV

9. John 7:5, NIrV

10. 2 Peter 1:16, NIrV

11. Matthew 14:21–22, NIrV

12. Campbell, Charlie H. *Archaeological Evidence for the Bible: Exciting Discoveries Verifying Persons, Places and Events in the Bible.* Carlsbad, California: The Always Be Ready Apologetics Ministry, 2012, page 127.

CHAPTER 11: AT THE CROSS

1. John 19:6, NIrV

2. John 19:7, NIrV

3. John 19:16, NIrV

4. John 19:25, NIrV

5. John 19:26, NIrV

6. John 19:27, NIrV

7. John 19:30, NIrV

8. Psalm 22:16, NIrV

9. "The Death of Peregrine, page 82," *Works of Lucian of Samosata*, May 6, 2013, http://sacred-texts.com/cla/luc/wl4/wl420.htm.

10. Matthew 26:53–54, NIrV

CHAPTER 12: A NEW BEGINNING

1. Luke 23:55, NIrV

2. Mark 16:6–7, NIrV

3. Acts 2:12, NIrV

4. Acts 2:32, NIrV

5. John 21:24, NIrV

6. James 1:1, NIrV

7. Jude 1:21, NIrV

8. "Antiquities of the Jews, 20.9.1," *The Works of Flavius Josephus*, May 6, 2013, http://www.sacred-texts.com/jud/josephus/ant–20.htm.

STUDENT RESOURCES

Blankenbaker, Frances. *What the Bible Is All About for Young Explorers.* Ventura, California: Regal Books, 1986.

Dowley, Tim. *The Student Bible Atlas.* Minneapolis: Augsburg, 1996.

Ham, Ken with Cindy Malott, *The Answers Book for Kids, Volume 1: 22 Questions from Kids on Creation and the Fall.* Green Forest, Arizona: Master Books, 2008.

Ham, Ken with Cindy Malott, *The Answers Book for Kids, Volume 3: 22 Questions from Kids on God and the Bible.* Green Forest, Arizona: Master Books, 2009.

Ham, Ken with Cindy Malott, *The Answers Book for Kids, Volume 4: 22 Questions from Kids on Sin, Salvation, and the Christian Life.* Green Forest, Arizona: Master Books, 2009.

McDowell, Josh and Sean McDowell. *Jesus is Alive! Evidence for the Resurrection for Kids.* Ventura, California: Regal, 2009.

Osborne, Rick and K. Christie Bowler. *I Want to Know About God, Jesus, the Bible, and Prayer.* Grand Rapids, Michigan: Zonderkidz, 2000.

Strobel, Lee with Rob Suggs and Robert Elmer. *Case for Christ for Kids.* Grand Rapids, Michigan: Zonderkidz, 2010.

Van der Maas, Ruth, Marnie Wooding, and Rick Osborne. *Kid Atlas: Important Places in the Bible and Where to Find Them.* Grand Rapids, Michigan: Zonderkidz, 2002.

Water, Mark. *The Big Book About Jesus.* Nashville: Thomas Nelson Publishers, 1995.

Water, Mark. *The Big Book of Bible People.* Nashville: Thomas Nelson Publishers, 1996.

ABOUT THE AUTHOR

Nancy I. Sanders is the bestselling children's author of over 80 books including *Old Testament Days: An Activity Guide* with over 80 hands-on projects. Her award-winning nonfiction children's books include *D is for Drinking Gourd: An African American Alphabet*, *America's Black Founders*, and *Frederick Douglass for Kids*. Nancy delights in making history come alive to young readers. She lives with her husband, Jeff, and their two cats in sunny southern California. Nancy and Jeff have two grown sons, Dan and Ben (with his lovely wife Christina). Visit Nancy's website at www.nancyisanders.com.